Patriotic Primer

By Wesley Schaum

Schaum's Pathway to Musicianship

The *Schaum Making Music Piano Library* integrates method, theory, technic and note reading with appealing materials for recital and repertoire. Schaum's well-proven motivational philosophy and sound pedagogy are widely recognized.

Foreword

This book is designed to make familiar patriotic music as easy as possible. A student with just six to eight weeks study will be able to start enjoying this album.

The pieces are arranged in five-finger position with melody divided between the hands. A minimum of finger numbers is used. Large, widely spaced notes help make music reading easier. Rests have been purposely omitted so the student can focus on the notes.

Duet accompaniments offer many possibilities for recitals and school events. The duets help provide rhythmic training and ensemble experience especially valuable to beginners. The person playing the accompaniment is free to add pedal according to his/her own taste.

The duets are recommended for use at home as well as at the lesson. However, the student should work alone at first until the notes and rhythm of the solo part are secure.

Index

Exclusively Distributed By

HAL•LEONARD® CORPORATION
7777 W. BLUEMOUND RD. P.O. BOX 13819 MILWAUKEE, WI 53213

ISBN-13: 978-1-62906-079-8

Marines' Hymn

Allegro

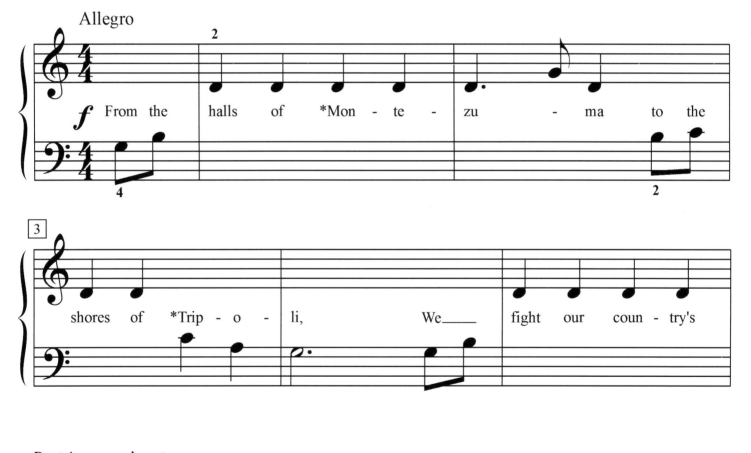

From the halls of *Mon - te - zu - ma to the shores of *Trip - o - li, We___ fight our coun - try's

Duet Accompaniment

Teacher's Note: If the pupil is in the early grades in school and has not yet had fractions, do not attempt to explain the dotted quarter notes and eighth notes. The rule to follow is this: *experience should precede explanation.* Teach the rhythm by rote. Delay the explanation until the situation arises at a later time when the student has acquired fraction readiness.

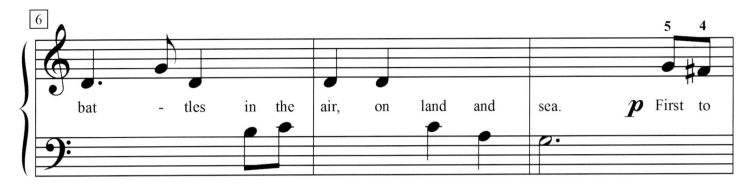

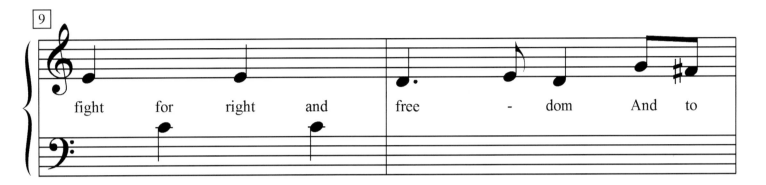

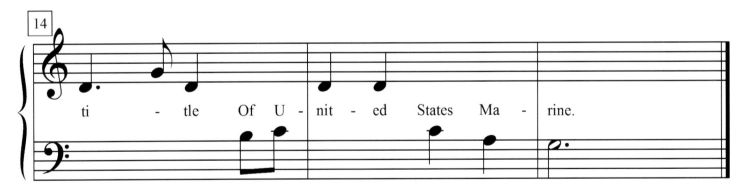

Duet Accompaniment (continued)

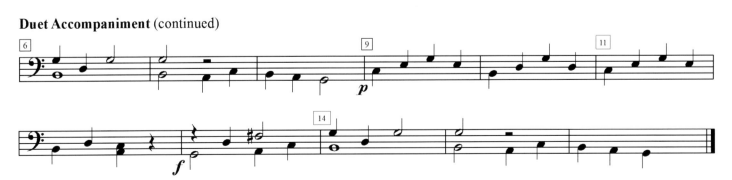

* *Montezuma* is the royal palace in Mexico City. *Tripoli* is the capital of Lybia, a north African country.

4

America

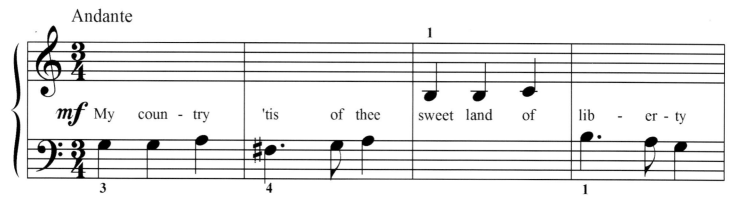

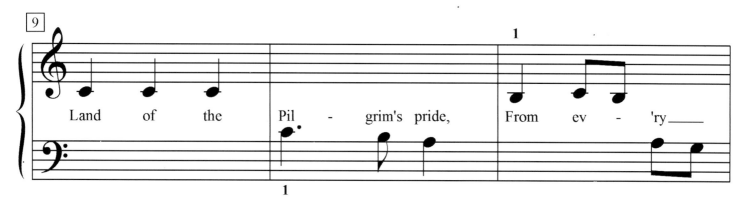

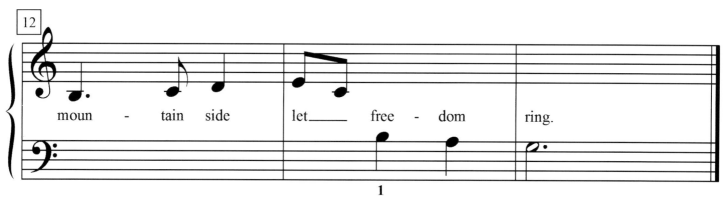

Duet Accompaniment (Stem Up = R.H. Stem Down = L.H.)

Yankee Doodle

Giocoso

f Fath'r and I went down to camp, A - long with Cap - tain Good - 'in, And

there we saw the men and boys As thick as has - ty pud - din'.

Yan - kee Doo - dle keep it up, Yan - kee Doo - dle dan - dy,

Mind the mu - sic and the step, and with the girls be han - dy.

Duet Accompaniment

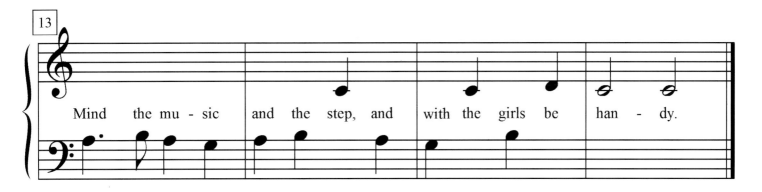

Battle Hymn of the Republic

Maestoso

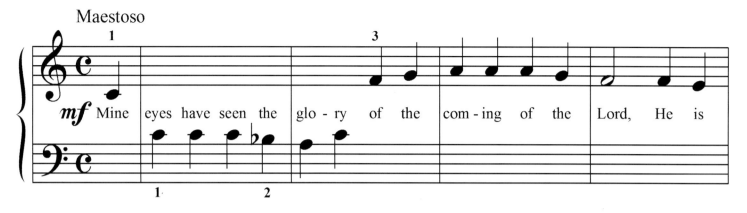

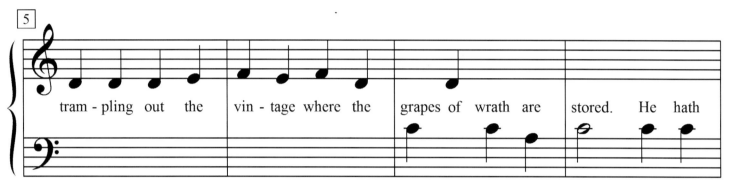

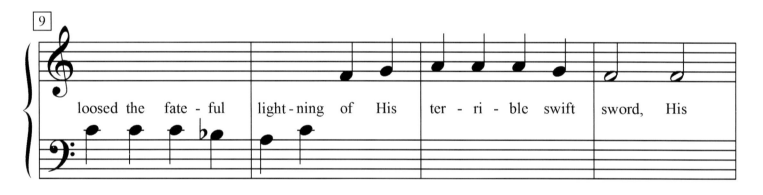

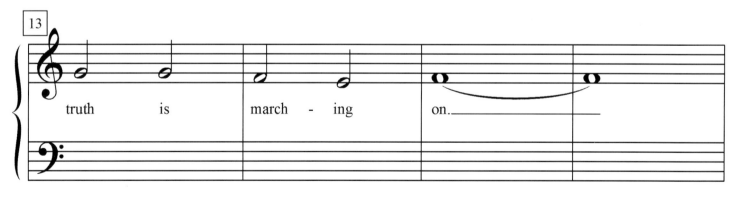

Duet Accompaniment

Teachers Note: Each pair of quarter notes, in solo and duet (1st + 2nd count and 3rd + 4th count in each measure) may be performed as a dotted rhythm (dotted quarter + single 8th note) if desired. This may be taught to the student by rote.

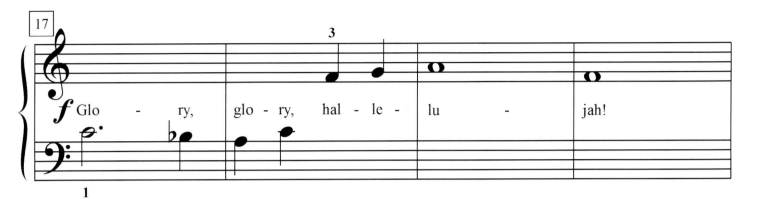

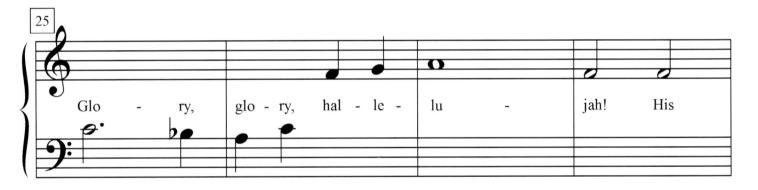

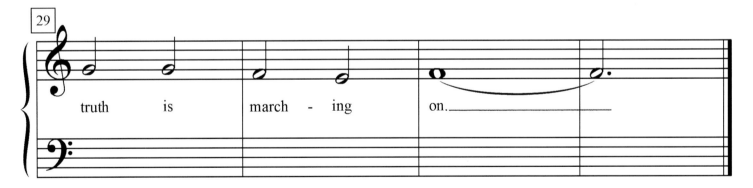

Duet Accompaniment (continued)

Yankee Doodle Dandy

Bravura

George M. Cohan

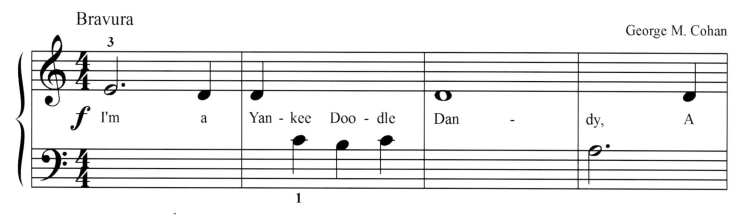

I'm a Yan - kee Doo - dle Dan - dy, A

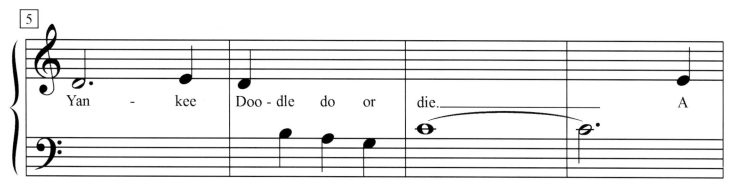

Yan - kee Doo - dle do or die._____ A

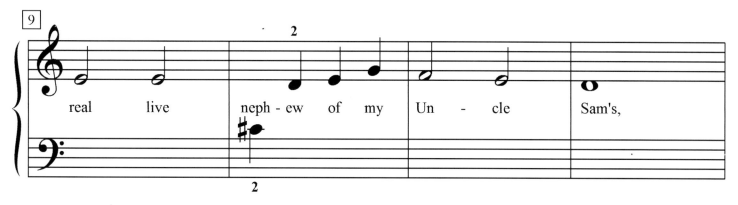

real live neph - ew of my Un - cle Sam's,

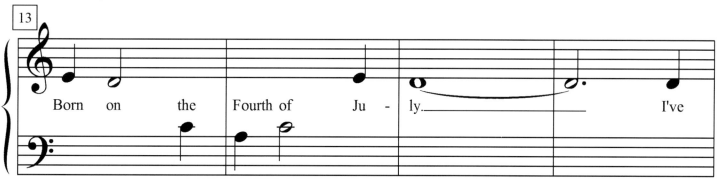

Born on the Fourth of Ju - ly._____ I've

Duet Accompaniment

9

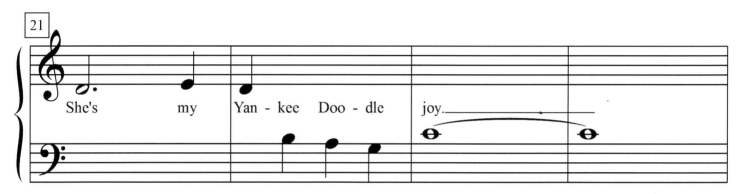

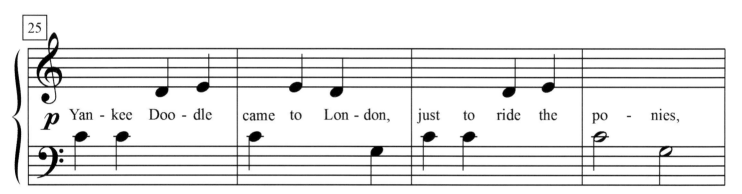

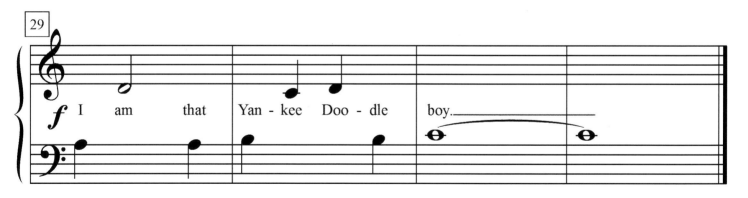

Duet Accompaniment (continued)

Caissons' Song

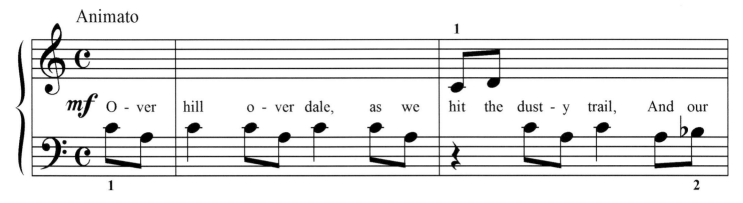

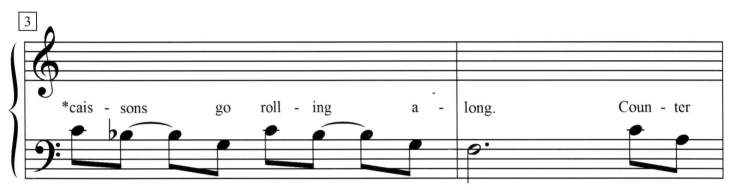

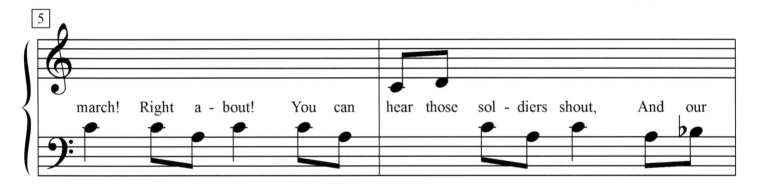

Duet Accompaniment

* *Caissons* (KAY-sahns) are wagons used to carry ammunition for army artillery pieces (cannons and other large guns). Caissons were originally pulled by horses and, in the early 1900's, by trucks. However, the modern army no longer uses caissons. This music has become the official song of the U.S. Army.

11

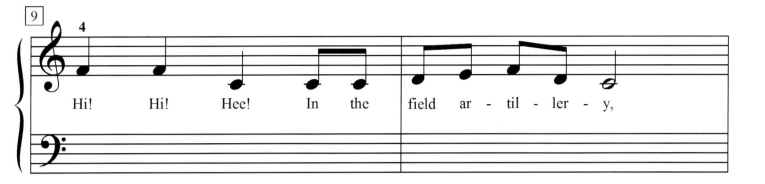

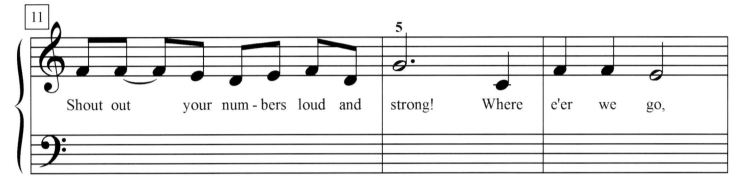

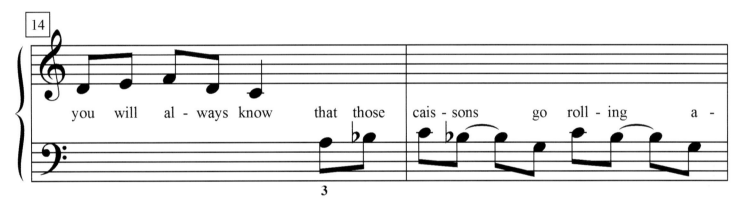

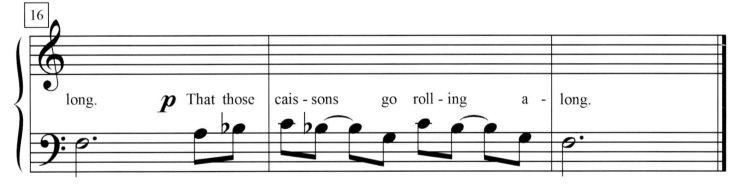

Duet Accompaniment (continued)

America the Beautiful

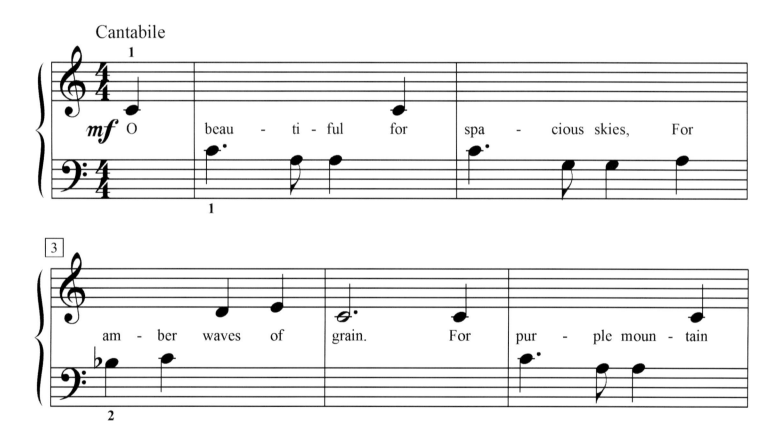

Cantabile

O beau - ti - ful for spa - cious skies, For am - ber waves of grain. For pur - ple moun - tain

Duet Accompaniment

13

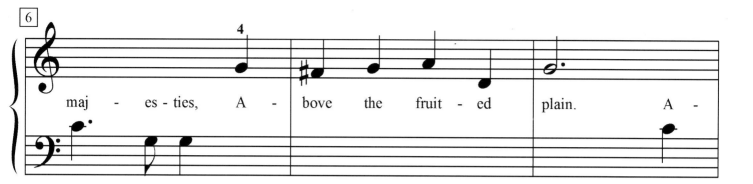

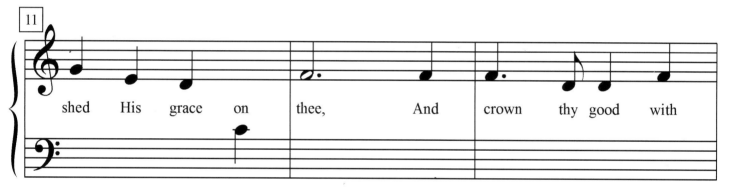

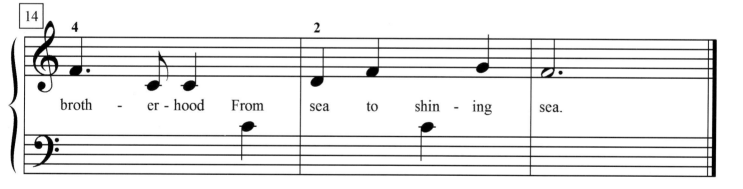

Duet Accompaniment (continued)

You're a Grand Old Flag

George M. Cohan

Spiritoso

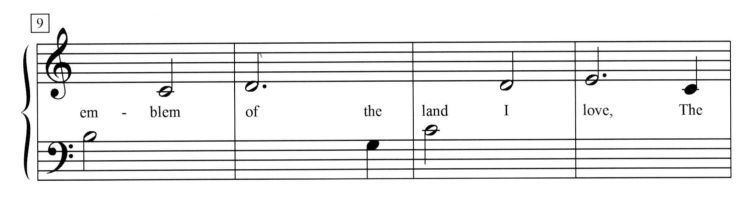

Duet Accompaniment

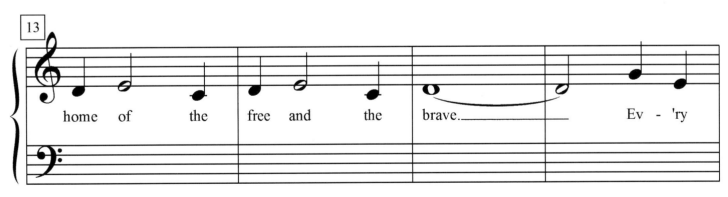

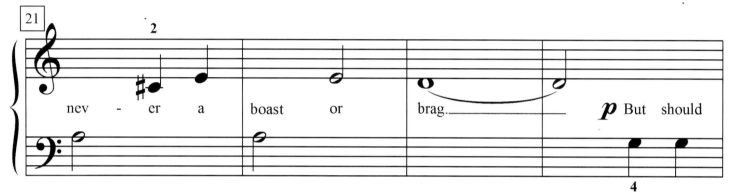

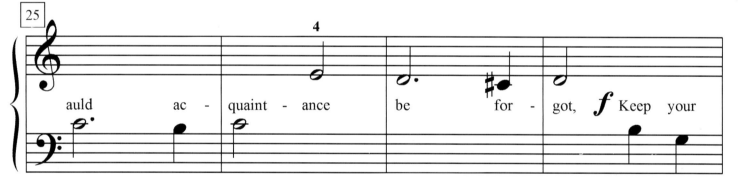

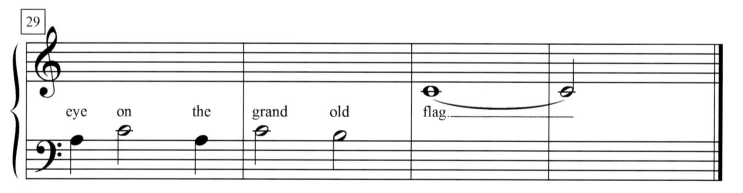

Duet Accompaniment (continued)

Stars and Stripes Forever

John Philip Sousa

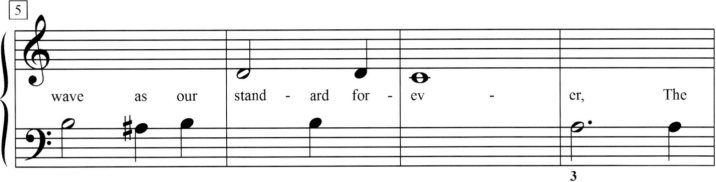

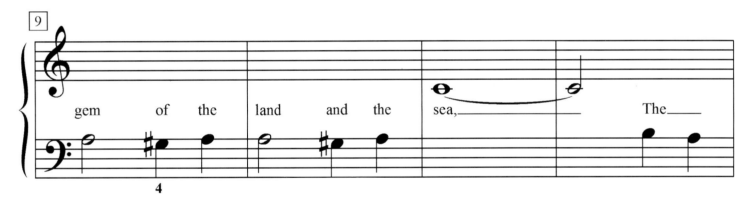

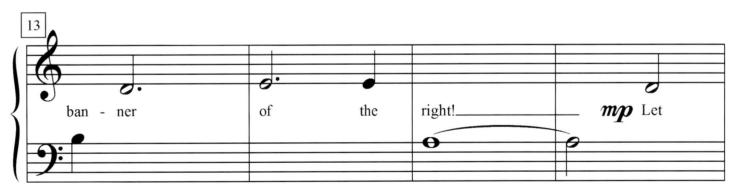

Duet Accompaniment

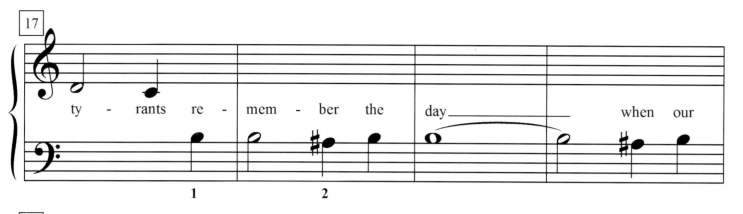

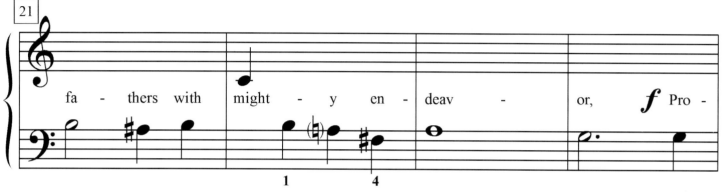

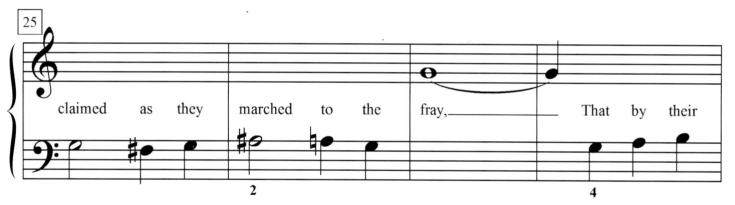

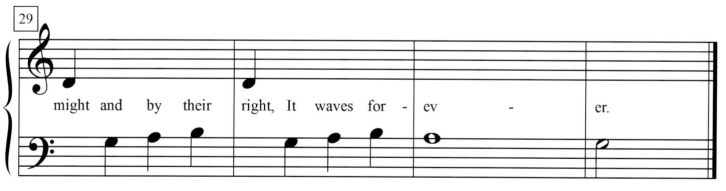

Duet Accompaniment (continued)

Hail to the Chief

Allegretto

Hail to the chief who in tri - umph ad - van - ces,

Hon - ored and bless'd be the ev - er - green___ pine!

Duet Accompaniment

This is the "official march" of the President of the United States. It is performed by military bands when the President appears for a formal visit or for official ceremonies.

Teacher's Note: The 8th notes in the solo part may be played in a dotted rhythm (dotted 8th + 16th). If so, the dotted rhythm should be taught by rote.

Long may the tree, in his ban - ner that glan - ces Flour - ish the shel - ter and

grace of our line! Hail to the chief who in tri - umph ad-van - ces,

mp

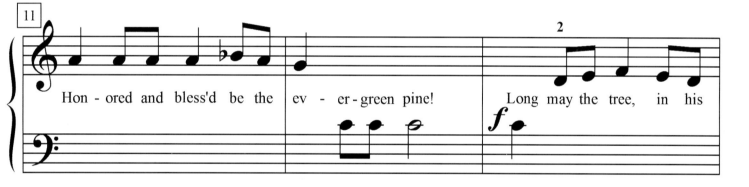

Hon - ored and bless'd be the ev - er-green pine! Long may the tree, in his

f

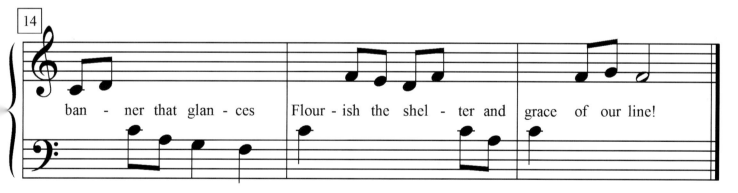

ban - ner that glan - ces Flour - ish the shel - ter and grace of our line!

Duet Accompaniment (continued)

Star Spangled Banner

Words by Francis Scott Key

Maestoso

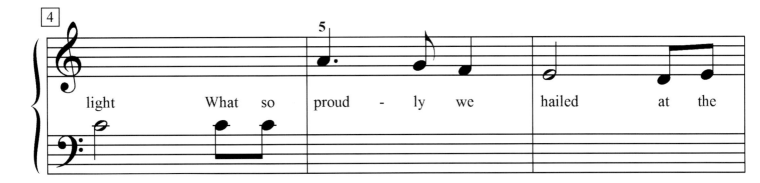

O___ say can you see by the dawn's ear - ly

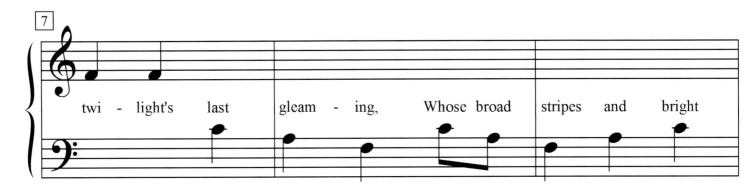

light What so proud - ly we hailed at the

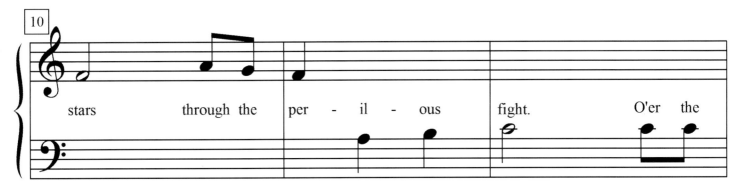

twi - light's last gleam - ing, Whose broad stripes and bright

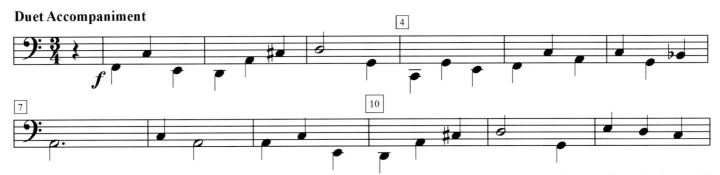

stars through the per - il - ous fight. O'er the

Duet Accompaniment

Teacher's Note: Some of the 8th notes, as appropriate, in the solo part may be played in a dotted rhythm (dotted 8th + 16th). If so, the dotted rhythm should be taught by rote.

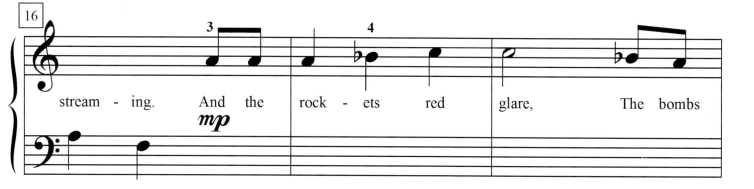

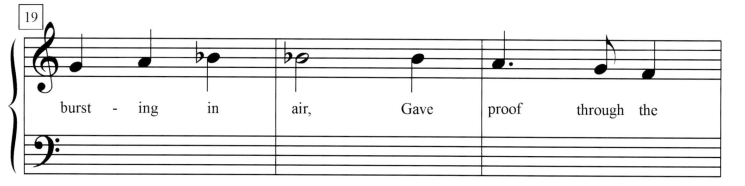

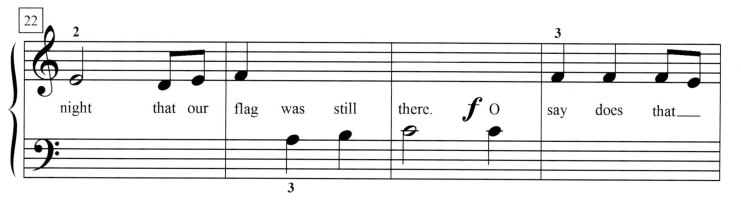

Duet Accompaniment (continued)

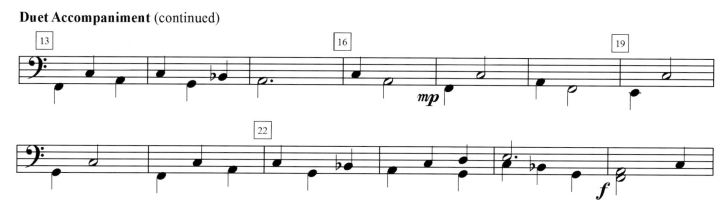

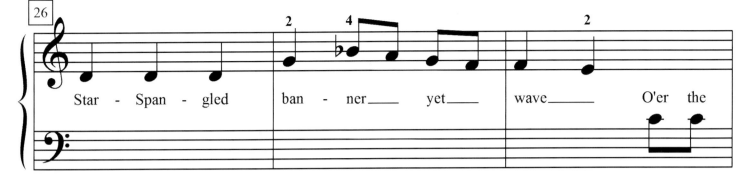

Duet Accompaniment (continued)

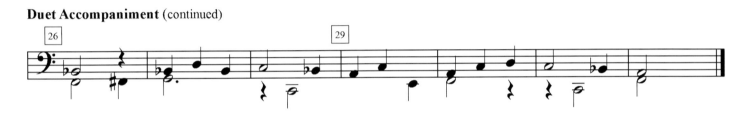

American Hymn

Larghetto

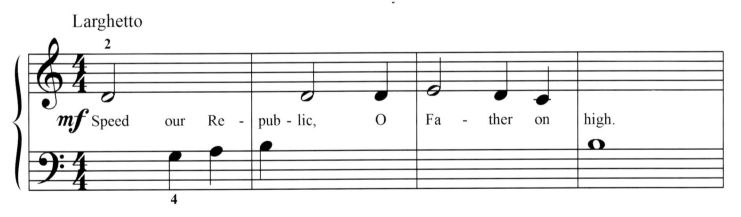

Duet Accompaniment

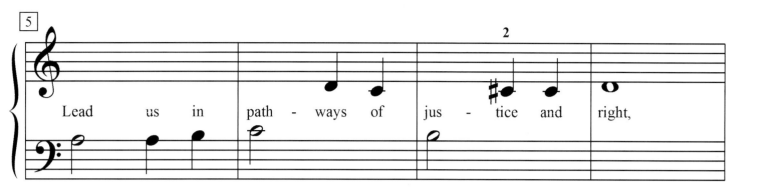

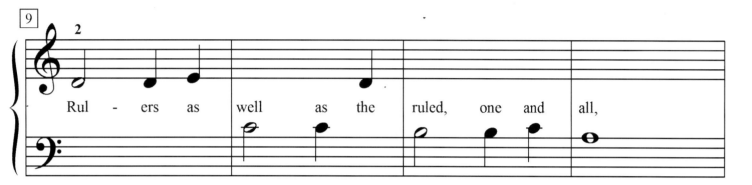

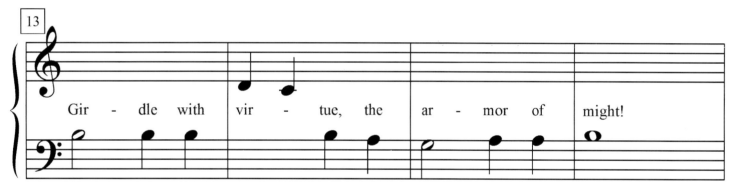

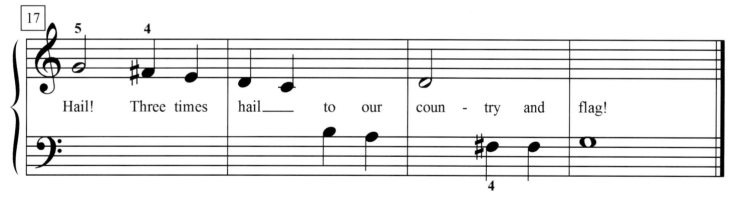

Duet Accompaniment (continued)